WRECK THE HALLS

Also by Jen Yates:

*Cake Wrecks:
When Professional Cakes Go
Hilariously Wrong*

WRECK THE HALLS

CAKE WRECKS GETS "FESTIVE"

Jen Yates

**Andrews McMeel
Publishing, LLC**
Kansas City · Sydney · London

Andrews McMeel Publishing, LLC
an Andrews McMeel Universal company
1130 Walnut Street, Kansas City, Missouri 64106

www.andrewsmcmeel.com

11 12 13 14 15 WKT 10 9 8 7 6 5 4 3 2 1

ISBN: 978-1-4494-0775-9

Library of Congress Control Number: 2011926172

Book design by Holly Ogden

Attention: Schools and Businesses
Andrews McMeel books are available at
quantity discounts with bulk purchase for
educational, business, or sales promotional use.
For information, please e-mail
the Andrews McMeel Publishing
Special Sales Department:
specialsales@amuniversal.com

Back in 2009, halfway through our first-ever book tour, my husband, John, ended up in a Dallas ER with a staph infection in his blood, severe pneumonia, and a lump on his head the size of a golf ball. (Ask him about that lump sometime; he loves telling the story.) Though his condition was severe enough to be life-threatening, John spent his time in ICU paradoxically taking care of everyone else: managing hotels and travel for me, rescheduling our shows, and assuring fans he was fine when he wasn't. At his insistence, we did our next show barely a week later, and with his lungs still 25 percent full of fluid.

I think it's safe to say that no one has ever suffered more in the name of goofy cakes than John, and for that, *this* book of goofy cakes is dedicated to him.

Now, sweetie, about our next tour . . .

Contents

Acknowledgments

When I wrote my first book, *Cake Wrecks*, I never could have dreamed I'd get to write another. So, first and foremost, thank you to everyone who purchased, read, and/or told their friends about "that funny cake book." Without you I'd have to get a *real* job.

This book also wouldn't exist without the contributions of wreckporters and wreckerators alike, and I'm deeply indebted to all the people out there armed with either cameras or piping bags, respectively. It's the circle of wreckage, my friends, and we all have our place. Even the people making cupcake cakes. [shudder]

Thanks also to my agent, Christopher Schelling, and all of the amazing people at Andrews McMeel—especially Amy Worley, Kathy Hilliard, my editor Chris Schillig, and Holly Ogden, whom I was thrilled to have back designing this book.

Somehow Cake Wrecks the blog survived even while I was knee-deep in holiday wreckage, due in large part to Jen Dorsman (aka Number1), Julianne Lau (aka Wrecky Minion), and Anne-Marie Carrier (aka Wrecksistant). You ladies rock my Wrecked world. Thank you.

Then there are the long-suffering friends and family who continue to put up with my antisocial, "on a deadline" ways, and occasionally even drag me out of the house to remind me what the sun looks like. These real drags include my parents, Jim and Sharon Yates; my mother-in-law, Donna; my brother, Ben; John and Abby Gjertsen; Mat and Amy Weiss, Ray Lau; my unofficial marketing manager, Sean DiMercurio; Chris Friend and Chad Eyer; Craig Jarrett; and all the rest of the Second Saturday gang who've cheered me on from the beginning.

Thanks also to Tim Moran, who beat me to the punch by suggesting *Wreck the Halls* for the title. I may never forgive you for that, Tim, but thanks.

And then there's John: husband, partner, coworker, cowriter, and co-keeping-me-saner. Though he made me do the actual writing (the taskmaster!), John poured hours and hours into this book's creation, and I'd never have finished it without him. Thanks, sweetie. I love you.

The Disclaimers

Helloooooo, Wreckies!

Well, here we are again. You, standing there with this book in your hands. Me, sitting here hoping you're standing there with this book in your hands. My cat, hacking up a hairball. It's like the circle of life, only with more desperation, wreckage, and cat vomit.

Good times.

Now, for those of you who have not had the pleasure of reading my previous book: Why not? Cease this mindless procrastination at once, and go forth and acquire said tome!

Or, just read the following disclaimers. Then you'll be all caught up.

DISCLAIMER #1: "A Cake Wreck is any professionally made cake that is unintentionally sad, silly, creepy, inappropriate—you name it. A Wreck is not necessarily a poorly made cake; it's simply one I find funny, for any number of reasons."

In other words: my book, my rules. If you find yourself disagreeing with my assessment of any of these Wrecks, a few quick blows about the head and neck with this book should set you right as rain.

DISCLAIMER #2: Much like horoscopes, rodeo clowns, and Pat Robertson, nothing in this book should be taken too seriously. I am not the consumer watchdog of cakes. Cake Wrecks is simply my way of finding the funny in unexpected, sugar-filled places. If you're offended by poo jokes or dripping sarcasm, see Disclaimer #1, paragraph 2.

DISCLAIMER #3: All of the photos in this book were taken and submitted by the brave Wreckporters of CakeWrecks.com. These intrepid crusaders are often forced to employ speed, stealth, and ancient camera phones to bag their bounty. As a result, some of these photos are less than professional-looking. The rest are downright crappy. We're very sorry. Deal with it. (Or see Disclaimer #1, paragraph 2.)

Okay, all caught up? Are you ready to WRECK?!

Or maybe just sit there and look at some funny cakes? Ah, I thought so. In that case: *you may proceed.*

Here We "Go"

It starts in October.

You know what I'm talking about: that nagging, weighty feeling of dread. The disquiet in the back of your mind. The suspicion that something, somewhere, is waiting to unleash a horror beyond your wildest imaginings.

Then, before you can say "spider goosing a ghost . . ."

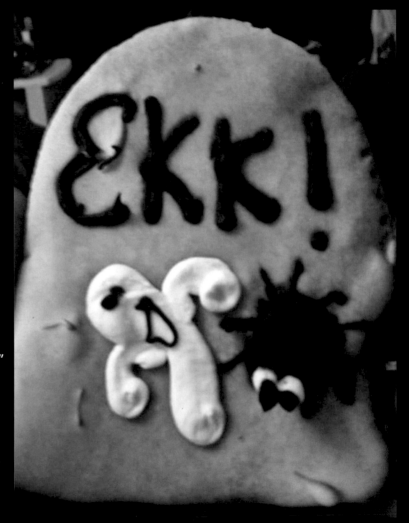

... *this* happens:

Candy Fun Cake

So, "Candy Fun Cake," we meet again.

"Ah, but Jim," you say—because this time you've forgotten both my name *and* my gender—"Jim, that's Halloween! It's *supposed* to have lots of ugly cakes and gross goodies! That's part of the fun!"

I suppose you have me there.

Ah, but—BUT—will you have me once we move on to *Thanksgiving*?

Exhibit A

Vampire Pilgrim

For some reason I was expecting
more sparkles.

Exhibit B

Circus Peanut Blow-Up Doll

There will be times in this book when your sanity will desire—nay, *demand*—some form of explanation, lest your sense of reality disintegrate into a gibbering pile of madness while you vainly try to ascribe meaning to a circus peanut dressed as Eve declaring it's "Time for thrunks."

To this I can only say: buckle up, bucko. You ain't seen *nothin'* yet.

Hey, I just call 'em like I see 'em.

And *speaking* of
smooth segues . . .

Look! Turkey!

Admittedly, he's looking a bit
more "goosed" right now.

Now, what we have *here* is what we refer to as a

FOCUSED, NONTERMINAL, REPEATING PHANTASM,

or a

CLASS 5 FULL-ROAMING VAPOR:

Chocolate

Real nasty one, too!

But before we go on, let's take a moment to learn the *real* history of Thanksgiving—and I don't mean that drivel they teach in "schools."

Take it away, bakers!

Here we see that Thanksgiving died in roughly 1620. It was a rocky start for the holiday, to be sure, but this grave situation teaches us to stay well grounded and never take *any* cake for granite.

Next let's meet Thanksgiving's
two favorite sidekicks.

Jesus:

"HOW . . .
did I end up with blue eyes, again? Just curious."

And pilgrim ringleader

Zaphod,

the evil overeater with tiny T-rex arms and a heart of gold:

"We come bearing water balloons.
Or possibly avocados."

Together these brave individuals forged a whole new world* of peace, prosperity, and ridiculously large turkey skirts.

"Fabulous, Harry, I love the feathers."

*That's where we'll beeee!

Of course, no one really knows where the cornucopia, or horn of plenty, originated, but if this cake is any indication . . .

. . . then I'd say Mel Gibson had something to do with it.

So, where did the tradition of *eating* turkeys come from? Well, as this model clearly demonstrates:

. . . once Zaphod hooked the bird up to seven freshly pickled hearts with telephone cords, they were only a single lightning strike away from the New World's first Horcrux.

And there was *much* rejoicing.

Whew! All this history can be *exhausting*, don't you think? That's why I, for one, prefer plain ol' "turkey day" over "Thanksgiving." That way, instead of tedious gratitude-exercising rituals, we can focus on the really *important* things.

You know, like football.

And cheering on our "super bowel." (*Go! Go! Go!*)

Bummer.

Getting back to "turkey day," though, on second thought maybe that's a little too obvious. We need something that *says* "turkey" without spelling it out, you know? Something catchy. Something fun. Something . . . misspelled.

This works.

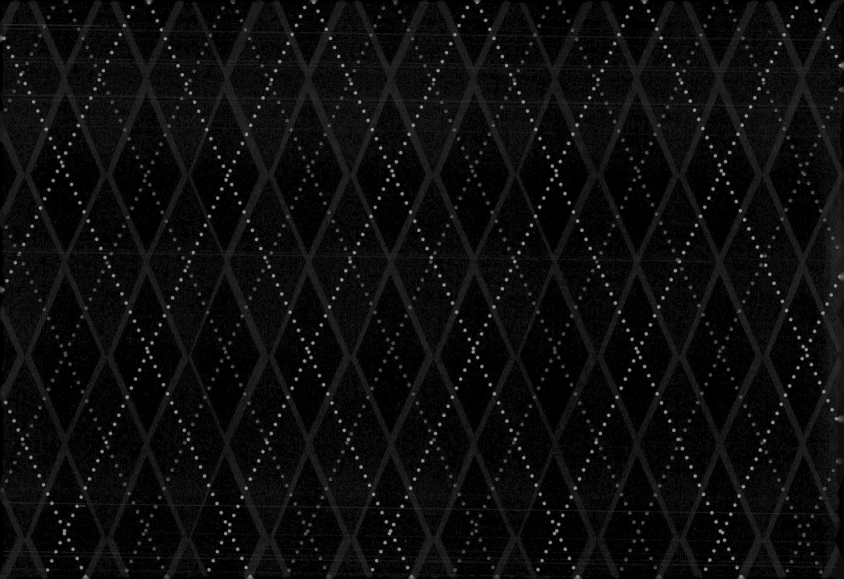

Let's Talk Turkey

Cooking, to me, is kind of like giving a constipated badger a prostate exam: Even if I *could* do it, why would I *want* to? That's what McDonald's is for. (The cooking, I mean. Not so much the badger prostate exams. [Note to self: work on segues.])

However, like all Americans, I believe that once I have seen something on TV, I am fully qualified to write a book about it. Which is why I am now going to teach you everything you need to know about cooking your holiday turkey. Because I care. And I think I saw this on *Wild Kingdom* once. And also I'm being paid.

CHOOSE YOUR TURKEY

If you don't have a school of turkeys flapping about your front lawn—which gives you the luxury of picking off the most annoying one—you'll have to rely on your trusty neighborhood woodsman for this. (Remember to haggle. I hear they like beads, gin, and back issues of *Cosmo*.)

Odds are your woodsman will bring back a variety of turkeys. Here are a few helpful tips when choosing yours.

Make sure it is *actually* a bird and not the Great Old One Cthulhu, as this makes it much harder to pluck.

"I KILL YOU!"

Avoid turkeys with unusually swollen heads and/or improperly placed gizzards.

You'll never get any of the guys to carve.

Besides, this one looks a little cold.

Take your time! The last thing you want is a bird that ends up looking like crap.

Talk about a **party-pooper!**

This one's *totally* giving me the stink-eye.

PREPARE YOUR TURKEY

I find that a firm hand and liberal use of alcohol make this step go much smoother.

So, once you're thoroughly soused, look your bird in the eye and say:

"This is going to hurt. Sorry."

If you're feeling bad about this step, it may help to remember that turkeys are idiots.

"Da*HURRRR*"

REMOVE THE FEATHERS, GIZZARDS, AND FOOTBALL

Just yank.

When you're done,
the bird should look
like this:

So in other words:
embarrassed.

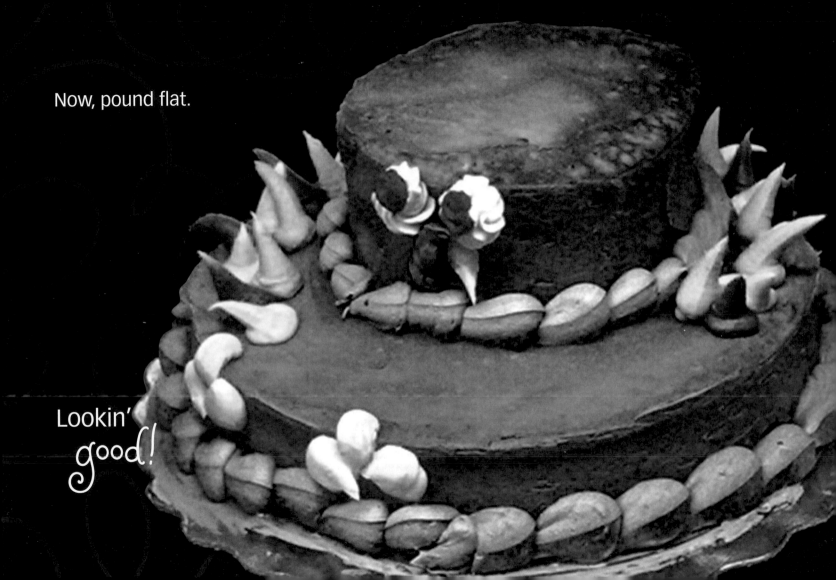

Now, pound flat.

Lookin' *good!*

STUFF YOUR TURKEY

Alpo or Fancy Feast works great for this.

But not *too* much:

What goes down must come up!

COOK YOUR TURKEY

Microwave times can vary, so it's important to program yours correctly. I like to go with the "popcorn" setting. Figure one bag per pound, so 15 pounds of turkey = 15 bags of popcorn. See? Easy peasy!

You'll know your turkey is done when you hear a small explosion. And the smoke alarm goes off.

Or, if you prefer your bird slightly *less* well done, simply remove at the hard crack stage.

"Putting the 'butt' in 'butterball' since 1875."

SERVE YOUR TURKEY

I like the classic "splayed on a bed of field greens," but feel free to choose whichever pose works best with your decor.

Now, tuck in! Just remember, the *best* part comes later. You know what I'm talking about: the night after, when, bleary-eyed and plagued with the munchies, you tiptoe out to the kitchen in your jammies. There you'll ease open the fridge, inhale deeply, and gaze with wonder at the delicious bounty awaiting you:

Mmmmm. Leftovers.

It's All Relative

There's no place like home for the holidays. Except maybe a vat of freshly squeezed lemonade when you're covered head to toe in paper cuts. BWAHAHA! Am I right? High five!

(Oh, c'mon, Mom, it was a joke! Just a . . . hey, now, PUT STAY PUFT DOWN.)

Toy hostages aside, though, I have to say I really loathe family gatherings.

Love. I really LOVE family gatherings.

Besides, what's *not* to love about sharing quality time with the people indirectly responsible for *every good* therapy session you've ever had?

It's almost like he's part of the family!

And once you look at it in that light, I think you'll agree that these seasonal gatherings are an *excellent* time to bring up all those childhood grievances and awkward birthday traumas.

Sean: [attempting to point and failing] "Who's greater now, Mom and Dad? HUH? WHO'S GREATER NOW?!?" [sobbing]

Alexandria: "Seconds on pie, anyone?"

"For the last time, Aunt Beth, I am NOT 'dying of loneliness.' Not everyone wants to get married, you know!

"And you can keep the ferrets."

And what family memory book is complete without a little passive-aggressive affection?

Thanks for the cake, Grandpa Joey! *I hate you.*

Not that it's *all* bad, of course. Every family trip down memory lane also has its good times:

It's
Food~Stamp
Day !!

The milestones
to celebrate . . .

Congratulations
High School
Dropout

Needless to say, Lucy's sixth-grade biology class was *thrilled* with their lunchtime treat.

And, of course, the welcoming of *new* members into the family:

So for all these great and grating memories, be sure to use your time together
as a family to express some warm and heartfelt appreciation.

And, guys? *I mean that.*

Black Friday

In order to prevent all that tedious goodwill and Thanksgiving-ish gratitude from bleeding into the weekend, American vendors made the next day *another* holiday. A holiday that is, in essence, the opposite of Thanksgiving. A yin to Thanksgiving's yang, if you will. A Walter Peck to its Peter Venkman. An Internet Explorer 6 to its, well, anything.

It's called Black Friday.

This is a day when we, the sound-minded consumers, spend our hard-earned vacation time camping out on sidewalks so we can later engage in WWF-style grappling with *other* sound-minded consumers over who gets to pay $147.99 for the last Slap-Me-Silly SpongeBob.

Sound-minded consumer: "Drop the doll, Grandpa, or so help me I'll take out the *other* hip!"

Other sound-minded consumer: [using walker as a battering ram] "It's not a doll, it's an INTERACTIVE ACTION FIGURE!!"

Tiny Tim: "And God bless us, everAAAUUUGGHHHH!!" [being run over by rioting sound-minded consumers]

Yep, for some reason it always comes down to the toys, doesn't it?
I mean, sure, there are always a few electronical doo-dads that the guys go gaga for . . .

It's an iPod Shuffle. *Obviously.*

. . . but the fists *really* start flying when parents contemplate disappointing their sweet little angels. Or, for that matter, their *children*.

And that's why I'm here with the nation's Wreckerators to recommend another way. A better way. A somewhat-but-not-entirely-copyright-infringing way.

That's right, I'm talking . . . *cheap knockoffs*.

Sure, you might end up with Shamwow Steve here:

HE'S CRAZY!
HE'S FUN!

And now,

HE'S MORE ABSORBENT!

Or DOREEN, THE GIRL WHO TRAVELS TO PLACES AND ASKS QUESTIONS YOU NEVER GET TO ANSWER™:

"Can *you* say '*pato cara*'?"

"Paa . . . tow . . ."

"*Muy bien*! I knew you could do it!"

"But I didn't . . ."

"Can *you* say '*por favor mantengase alejado de las puertas*'?"

"Um, maybe if you slowed down just a . . ."

"*Vamonos!* I see something more interesting than you over *there*!"

But, c'mon. How much are your kids *really* going to notice?

Ok, this
they
might
notice.

Still, just because the Tink Tank has packed on a few extra pounds:

Happy Birthday Alyssa

Tink noticed it was taking a lot more pixie dust than usual to get off the ground these days. Peter, wisely, said nothing.

... or Permanent Press Man looks, er, permanently pressed ...

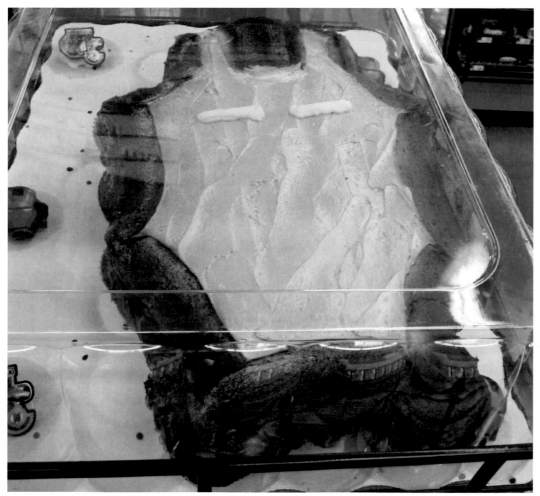

... is no reason to miss out on saving some dough!*

*My apologies for that half-baked "dough" pun. It goes against the grain to loaf around like that, but getting a rise out of you seems the yeast I can do when I'm on a roll. And donut forget: when a floury toast goes a-rye, crumby puns are second to naan! (Even though I get a bun wrap for being crusty, no matter how you slice it, *I ain't no challah-back girl.*)

Now baguette up, bee-yotches, 'cuz that's seventeen puns! *Woo woo!*

Besides, as Hollywood has proven time and time again with gems like *Wild Wild West* and *The Dukes of Hazzard*, sometimes we *need* newer versions to freshen up the old, boring, "time-honored classic" ones.

Take **Sir Stuffs-A-Lot, the "Flair Bear,"** here:

No, really. Take him. He's giving me the willies.

Ahem.

Or say your teenage niece* is obsessed with both hunky werewolves *and* classic cartoons. Why not combine the two?

Scooby Doo? *Were* are you?!?

"A rooby rooby RAWRRR!!"

*It's okay, ladies. We know you're just buying that book/movie/limited-edition shirtless Jacob and Edward doll set for "your niece." [wink wink]

You do have to be careful, though; if the "fun new look!" of your child's favorite character is a little *too* fun and new, you run the risk of said child not recognizing aforementioned character.

And then you're *really* screwed.

Child: "That's not Mickey Mouse."
You: "Yes, it is."
Child: "No, it's not."
You: "Well, it's *supposed* to be. How about we *pretend* it's Mickey?"
Child: "But it's *not.*"
You: "Okay, FINE, I'll buy you a pony! Just stop crying. Please?"

As you can see, this is not the ideal gift-giving situation. You may have saved a few bucks in the short term, but you've got a yard full of pony poo for the long haul. Not good.

The good news is you can never go wrong with anything educational:

Trust me.

Danger: High Yuletide

As we near the month of December, bakeries begin trying to make their designs more "season-appropriate."

Which is why it is at this time that you'll find, for example, the army toys attacking giant poinsettias:

"CALL IN BACKUP! WE NEED MORE *silly string!"*

Oh Oh Oh is right.

And of course, that perennial holiday favorite:

The Puppy-Pecking Parasite of Pastries Past!

It's a **deer tick.**

Get it? Huh?

Oh, quit groaning; that was freakin' *brilliant* on my part. Well worth the *doe* (assuming you only spent a coupla *bucks*).

Hey, you know how sometimes bakeries have those black holes that open up, creating dense heaps of frosting and flotsam so frightening that employees have to toss in the $27.99 price tag from a safe distance?

Well, it turns out they're not all bad;
sometimes the gravitational pull sucks in a
few handy household items.

Like lightbulbs.

Hey, wait a second . . .

WHY AREN'T MY LIGHTBULBS WORKING??

ATTENCION
THIS LIGTH BULBS
IS ONLY DECORATION

Oh.

Sure, NOW
you tell us.

Chalk it up to boredom, cluelessness, or excessive eggnog, but for some reason it's only when the weather turns colder that Wreckerators break out their most "creative" designs.

Here are a few of my favorites:

"Windows to the Soul"

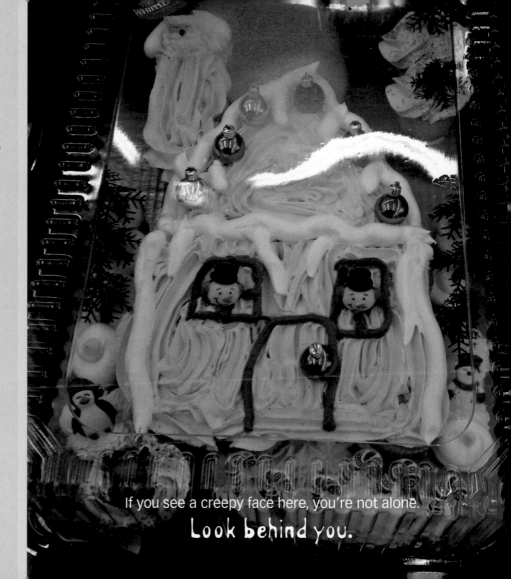

If you see a creepy face here, you're not alone.
Look behind you.

"Oh Tannen Bum"

Oh Tannenbum,
oh Tannenbum!
How cheeky are
your branches!

"The Yule Tidal Wave"

"Break Time!"

(Just out of frame is the Road Runner dust trail.)

I'm guessing "surf in snowman" is warning him about all those sea urchins coming in for the kill. "Surf in, snowman! *Surf in!*"

And speaking of bakers who hate snowmen, here's a cheery seasonal scene:

"AND THAT'S HOW FROSTY DIED, KIDS.

". . . CAKE?"

Or, for the new mom who has everything:

The Santa Breast Pump.

(I'd make a crack about how much it would suck not to serve this with milk, but I have the feeling you guys are waaay ahead of me.)

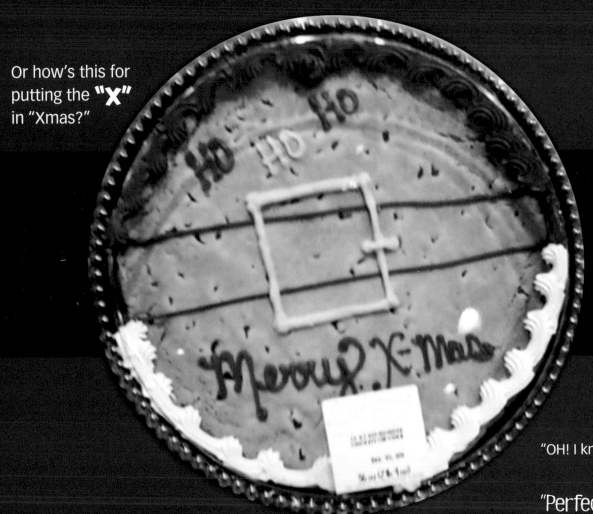

Or how's this for putting the **"X"** in "Xmas?"

"Gosh, if ONLY there was *some* way to make my edible X-mas Santa crotch a *little* more inappropriate.

"OH! I know! I'll add a 'ho ho ho.'

"Perfect!"

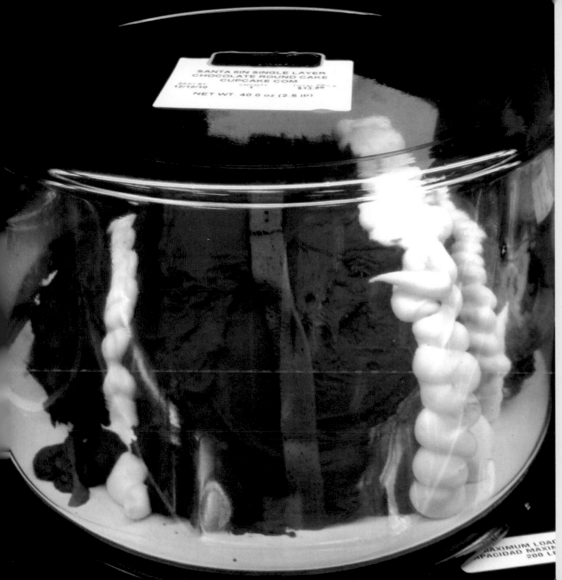

SANTA BIN SINGLE LAYER
CHOCOLATE ROUND CAKE
CUPCAKE COM

12/12/10

NET WT. 40.0 oz (2.5 lb)

MAXIMUM LOAD
CAPACIDAD MAXIM
200 LB

And finally, a holiday vignette that makes me feel like *singing*:

Here goes—
feel free to join in!

Santa got run over
by a snow plow,

Walking home from our
house Christmas Eve,

You may say there's no such
thing as Santa,

But once you see this stain
you may believe!

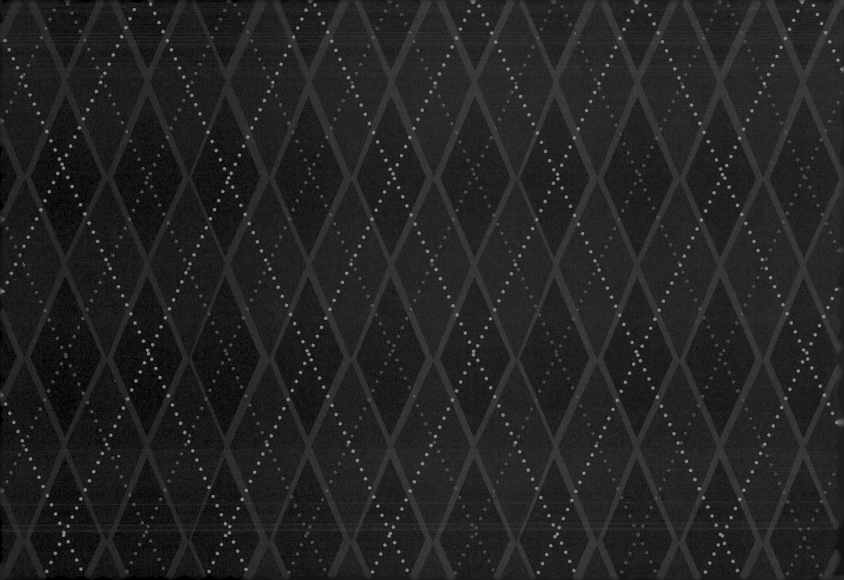

Child's Play

"Now let's check in with the Wreck n' Roll Bakery to meet the Kindergarten class responsible for these *charming* seasonal treats."

"First we have Billy—and, my, what a big boy he is, too! Now, Billy, why don't you tell us about your *adowable widdle* snowman?"

"Dude, I'm twenty-seven. What's with the baby talk?"

"Ha ha! And already a great sense of humor, too! Okay, Sarah, tell us: Did your parents help you write on *your* cake?"

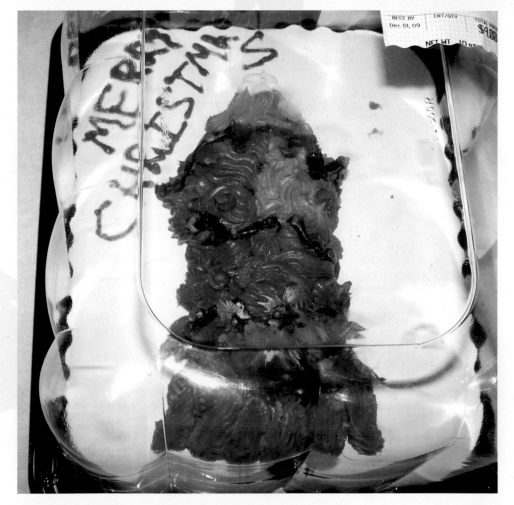

"No, I just asked my manager."

"I . . . see. Ah! And here's their manager now! Sheryl, I must say, your 'kids' here look really grown-up."

"They are. Except Wilhelm."

"Oh, is Wilhelm a child?"

"Nope, monkey. But he only handles the ribbon."

"Ohhhhkaaay. Wait. So, you're telling me that all these cakes . . .

. . . were made by *adult* bakers? Not five-year-olds?"

"Yup."

"And . . . they get *paid* for this?"

"Yup."

"With *money*?"

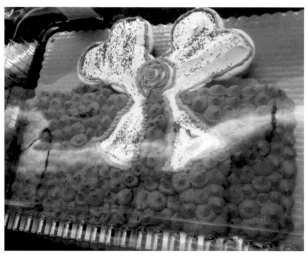

"Yup."

"I see. And just one last question, if you don't mind my asking: *Are you hiring?*"

"Sorry, can't help you right now. I'm on break."

"Well, there you have it, folks! And you all thought it was hard to find a job these days. *Pfffaw!*"

("Just to be clear, that 'Pfffaw!' wasn't me. It was Wilhelm. He ran out of ribbon.")

"Bad Wilhelm! *Baaaaad!*"

[Mr. Bill voice]
"Ohh nooo!"

"It all happened so *fast*. One minute I'm squatting in the woods, the next, *no arms*!"

Authorities are asking anyone with information on these crimes to call the bakery tip line at 555-MOSTLY-ARMLESS.

The rest of us are advised to be on the lookout for suspicious-looking arms dealers.

"Psst. Buddy. You interested? I've got a half-off special going: today it'll only cost you a leg."

We now return you to your regularly scheduled joke-fest.

"... so I say to the guy, okay, the clown can stay, but the Ferengi in the elf suit has to go!

"AHAHAHA!!

"Anyway, folks, that's it from the Wreck 'n' Roll Bakery. G'nite!"

Ode to a Sprig of Green Mistletoe I Found in My Armpit One Mid-Winter Morning

Ahem hem hem.

[dramatically]

Spriggy, spriggy, spriggy!
Mistle spriggy. Spristle Migg.
Pituitary morning!
Spidwinter, groaning udder!
Mistletoe? Really?
Really. Mistletoe.
Not even a particularly
Nice shade of green.

Chappy Chanukah!

Jews. They're just like you, only Jewish. (Unless *you're* Jewish, of course, in which case they're *exactly* like you.)
And like you, Jews have holidays that they celebrate, except theirs are a lot harder to spell.
Like "Passover." And "yarmulke." And "Mazel tov, Mordecai!"

Oy.

By the way, this
would be a good
place to mention
that I'm actually an
Orthodox Jew, born
and raised in Israel.

So it's a real shame
that's not the case.

Still, you should know that I *am* Jewish on my mom's side—the only side that counts—and I've been to Israel and had fish for breakfast and everything. So it is only with the deepest respect and admiration that I tell you I still don't know how to spell "Channukah."

[snort] Yeah. Like *THAT's* right.

Now Hannukkah (aka Channuka, Hannnukkah, Channnukkkka, or "Jewish Christmas") has been around for a very long time. It celebrates a beautiful miracle of light, life, and cultural identity.

Naturally, Wreckerators see this as a challenge.

Now, let's give credit where it's due: it's not easy to make a menorah look like the Holy Grail. In fact, you might say the person who bought these cookies "chose . . . *poorly.*" Then you might make a joke about the person's face melting off—much like this icing—when they open the package. Because even though that's the wrong movie, *it's still funny.*

HOLIDAY COOKIES

TOTAL PRICE
$2.69

Complicating matters further is the fact that Hannuka has very few associated symbols for bakers to wreck. Where Christmas has trees, reindeer, angels, hay troughs, etc., Hannuaka really only has two things: menorahs and stars.

Still, our industrious Wreckerators do what they can. Take this handy design, for example:

I'd give it nine thumbs up.

Or how about
"The Teal Tornado?"

And to think: *this was the one deemed most display-worthy.*

Now, who wants to play "Chest Cavity Chanikka"?

C'mon, you know you do! Setting fire to an alien rib cage has *never* been more festive.

Of course, even more common than the menorah around this time of year is the traditional Star of David.

Or, as some bakeries know them, "Christmas Stars."

"YO, BILL! GRAB ANOTHER TUB OF CHRISTMAS STARS, WILL YA? THIS MANGER SCENE NEEDS A SKY!"

Now, you might think that drawing a simple six-sided star on a cake would be easy.

You might also be an idiot.

Okay, I know what you're thinking—and I'd like to assure you that monkeys simply do not *like* tutus, much less yodeling, so your plan is patently useless.

However, getting back to this cake: for those of you protesting that it's simply not *possible* that it was supposed to be a Hunnakah cake . . .

You were saying?

I espccially like
this pairing:

**The
Hanukkah
Pentagram:**

"Ticking off just about
everyone since 2010."

To be fair, I should tell you the confusion works both ways.
For example, did you know that the Dallas Cowboys' logo is a five-pointed star?

Yeah. Neither did this baker.

Puts a whole new meaning to "throwing around the ol' pigskin," though, huh?

CHOCOLATE CHEWS   0.69   ALMOND CANOE

And also to be fair, I should note that some bakers think the Star of David is what pirates use to navigate during winter.

"Arr, where be me YARRmulke? I needs to be gettin' a reading on me starrr o' David!"

As a result, most bakeries have reached the sensible, sensitive solution to stop butchering sacred religious imagery with icing . . .

. . . and do it with *plastic* instead.

Well played, bakers. *Well played.*

Holiday
Wreck Creation

As you know, some bakers don't celebrate Christmas. Or Hanukkah. Or Kwanzaa. Or any other winter holiday. Heck, some don't even like *winter* all that much. Or snow. Or puppies.

Basically, there's just no making them happy.

So what do these noncelebratory, merriness-disadvantaged bakers do when forced to decorate holiday cakes by "the man" (aka "shift manager Sheryl")? They protest, of course! And *how* do they protest? In the conveniently labeled Four Stages of Holiday Wreck Creation, naturally!

What are these stages? And who labeled them so conveniently? For that matter, where am I even going with this chapter?

These are all excellent questions, and frankly, I have no idea how to answer any of them. But that won't stop me from making stuff up. Join me, won't you?

STAGE 1: DENIAL

Initially the baker refuses to acknowledge even the existence of the holiday season. Symptoms include repeatedly asking, "Happy *what* now?" and writing increasingly bizarre inscriptions on coworkers' stock holiday designs.

Eventually this may culminate in the invention of substitute holidays, which the decorator will insist are still celebrated "in the old country."

"Then we pay alms to the peppermint prince, and the next morning all the chamber pots are filled with

CANDY CORN!

"You've really never heard of it?"

After a hasty consult with middle management, most bakers will learn to embrace their holiday decorating duties with all the cheer and good grace that only a formal reprimand can instill. Thus beginning . . .

The baker works cheerfully enough, but the cakes are soon riddled with subtle, "unintentional" mistakes:

"Oh, whoops, did I spell it wrong? Gee, I am *so sorry.*"

"I'm pretty sure that's how the manual says to do it."

"Wait. You're saying 'Butthead Santa' looks like a . . . a . . . [whispering] *rear end?* Really?

STAGE 3: PASSIVE AGGRESSION

No longer content with simple "mistakes"—especially since management and customers don't notice them anyway—the baker moves on to deliberately sabotaging his or her own work, hoping to make holiday cakes *so* vile that no customer would dare purchase them.

"I call this one 'Seasonal Sushi Strings.'"

"Elf Blood Bath"

"Now, *here's* a great one for you regular folk. In fact, I find that dumping large loads of icing on the rear end there really helps with the flow of holiday spirit, don't you? Yep. Nothing like throwing a few logs on the fire, pinching off some candied corn, and writing in the ol' diary, uh, I mean notebook. Of course, there is still a fee, see, so don't forget to pay on your way out!

"And in case I'm being too subtle:

THIS CAKE LOOKS LIKE POOP."

STAGE 4: NOT-SO-PASSIVE AGGRESSION

Driven to desperate measures by customers' unflagging enthusiasm for even their most wrecked holiday cakes, the baker begins concocting designs intended to worry his/her therapist, frighten young children, and make the Grinch himself shed another heart size.

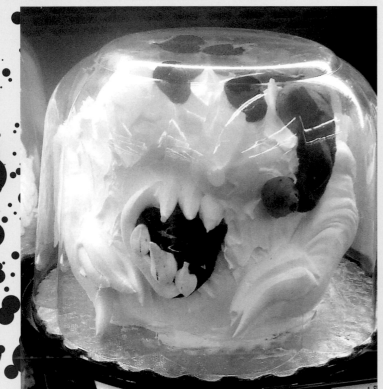

"Unless **ZOMBIE SANTA** claws his way out of the ground in time to terrorize you in your bedroom, that is."

"And this guy helps."

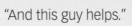

And so, my friends, in the infamous words of Barb Snodgrass, the veteran Wreckerator of the Saskatchewan Shop-A-Hock who pole-vaulted the counter one bleak December eve and rode the floor waxer out in a blaze of glory (or at least until the cops arrived):

Wax on, Barb. *Wax on.*

Winter, Underlined

Merry christ Mas

Marry Chritsmas C.E. 2.

Friends, vegans, countrypeople! The time again draws
nigh: a season of love, joy, peace, and goodwill toward
those who think the same way you do—why, I can
almost feel the warm fuzzies building toward critical
mass as I type. Won't you join me in a moment of fuzzy-
basking?

[basking] *Mmmm.*

Okay, enough of that. We have important matters to discuss.

Matters like: How the heck do we wish people a happy holiday without ticking them off?

I like it.

In fact, if you've been reading Cake Wrecks for a while, you may remember the famous Winter cake. It simply read, "WINTER," which was underlined. Now, that underline *clearly* conveyed a positive energy, and "Winter" neatly summed up the entire time period we're discussing, but some poo-pooing readers felt it was a bit . . . cold.

Well, *fine*, poo-pooers! In that case, how do you feel about . . .

THE ALBINO SPRINKLE BUSH OF JOY!?!

Eh? Now your cake recipients can simply *imagine* an underline-appropriate greeting.

Or, for you fast-and-loose, risk-taking types who want an actual "greeting" on your cake:

12 · Message
Cookie

Unit Price	Sell By	Net Wt/CT	Total Price
$7.19/lb	12/04/10	1	$8.99

20 oz (1 lb 4 oz)

See, instead of wishing someone happy *holidays*, which might be construed as offensive, you can wish them a happy *haliday*. The confusion this creates will give you ample time to either (A) escape, or (B) distract the person with an exuberant rendition of "*Stille Nacht*."*

Also don't forget the pink, navy, and mustard color scheme. It's "festive" and no one, without exception, will *ever* find it even *remotely* appetizing.

*Hand puppets optional, but recommended.

Or, if "haliday" isn't grabbing you in a platonically pleasing way, how about:

Perfect for your Spanish-speaking friends. Every day is an "hola!" day!

This one gets bonus points for "happe"; now no one can accuse you of telling them how to feel!

At this point I think I've forgotten how it's spelled.

Mission: **ACCOMPLISHED.**

Or, to *really* confuse the heck out of 'em:

"Um . . . I don't understand. Is this some kind of holiday thing?"

[waving hand puppets] *"Stiiille naaaacht! Heiiiilege naaacht!"*

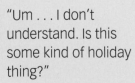

If you simply MUST wish someone a [whispering] *merry Christmas*,
then at least avoid offensive colors like red and green.

Also put a question mark after "Christmas," to communicate uncertainty
over the holiday's validity. You know, just to be safe.

There's also the snow globe approach:

12" MESSAGE COOKIE
BUTTERCREME ICING
$7.98
NET WT. 30oz (1.88lb)

Hm. Needs more sprinkles.

If you plan to illustrate your holiday cake, then please, be sensitive. Don't use off-putting imagery like angels, stars, trees, ornaments, babies, candy canes, fat men, reindeer, poinsettias, stockings, or the words "carrot cake."

Instead, go with things that *everyone* can agree on:

LIKE ALCOHOL.

Or gun-shop gingerbread houses.

Snowmen should always be made available
in a diverse range of colors:

FACT:

Whenever I see yellow snow, I always think, "You're in trouble, my peers!" And then I say it out loud, so I don't miss the joke.

Oh, and don't call them "snowmen." The correct term is "snowbeings."

So if you could stick some boobs on there somewhere, that'd be awesome.

Um . . .

**So tell me again:
WHERE did the customer ask you to write "Happy Birthday"?**

Hey, I know the holidays aren't always easy. Maybe you've got family in town. Maybe you have to work late. Maybe you've got tons of shopping to do, errands to run, and places to be, but not enough time to manage it all.

Or maybe—just maybe—you're trying to get your friend Roxanna a good-bye cake, but all the bakery has on hand are stock Christmas designs so you're forced to make do with one of those and hope the Wreckerator on duty doesn't screw up your instructions too badly.

But that's just a guess.

And that's why, at the end of the day, I think you'll agree that it's far easier to condense your holiday greetings back down to a single, all-purpose message:

Let it!

(Assuming you *like* snow, of course. If not . . . er . . . look! Hand puppets!)

WATCH ME BE A REBEL

My husband, John, tells me one cannot simply go stuffing sci-fi wreckage into a holiday-themed book. One has certain standards to uphold, after all. (And one has clearly never seen the wrecktastic Star Wars Holiday Special. C'mon. "Life Day"? Really?)

Anyway, to this I say, "PTTTHHHPPPT!"

No? Oh. My mistake.

Well regardless, I feel it is my duty to expose the true horror that is . . .

[DUN DUN *DUNNNN*]

. . . STAR-CROSSED WRECKAGE.

"NOOOOOO⋄⋄⋄OOOO⋄⋄OOo!"

[cradling hand]

Maybe that was a one-time oversight, though.
I mean, *surely* no self-respecting baker would ever intentionally . . . uh . . . oh no.

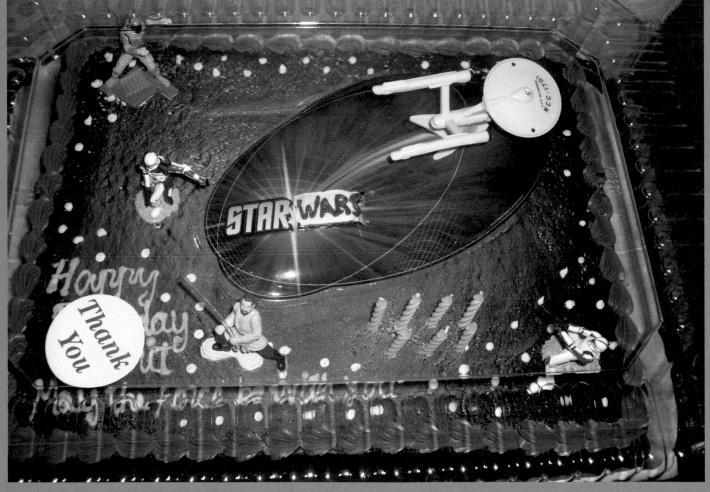

[head exploding]

Bakers, allow me to share with you the first rule of sci-fi:

DON'T CROSS THE STREAMS.

bakery

24 Ct Brownie Tray

$10.99

42 oz (2 lb 10 oz)

Unless of course you're trying to banish a transdimensional marshmallow mascot. Or maybe an ambulatory snowman.

In that case, have at it.

DID YOU KNOW?

1 John took my last name, Yates, when we got married.

2 "Yates" means "gate keeper."

3 We are total nerds.

(Ok, so you probably already knew #3.)

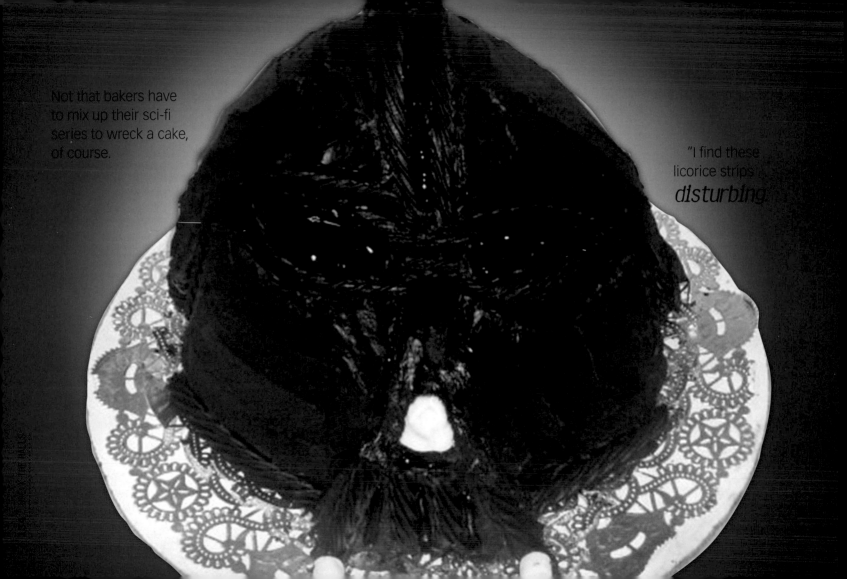

Not that bakers have to mix up their sci-fi series to wreck a cake, of course.

"I find these licorice strips *disturbing*"

To be fair, if *I* went "boldy" I'd probably use an alias, too.

Given all this star-crossed wreckage, you might think
you'd be better off ordering a generic "space" cake.

BWAHAHAHAAAA!

[wiping eyes] Hoo, WHEE! That's a good one. Seriously,
did you see how I typed that with a straight face?
Did ya? Hee. Ahee.

The following is a dramatic reenactment based on actual events:

Happy Birthday Jedi Adam

"Um . . . excuse me, why is this big blank circle here?"

"Lady, you ASKED for a 'space' cake. That's a big space."

Yes, really.

Piping my pain with their fingers,
Stinging my loves with their "words."
Baking them awf'ly—it's so wrong.
Baking them awf'ly! It's so wrong!
Filling me with strife; they're not nerds.
Baking them awf'ly. It's so wrong.

Well, my friends, I hope I've shed some light on the tragedy that is sci-fi mix-ups.

NOW, LIVE LONG, AND MAY THE FORCE BE WITH YOU.

Santa Scare Tactics

Parents, I give you an early Christmas present: a line up of Santa cakes so terrifying, even the naughtiest of children will run screaming to do the dishes.

"Well *helloooo,* children. I see you when you're sleeping."

"And I know when you're awake."

"I KNOW IF YOU'VE BEEN BAD OR GOOD, DIRTBAGS! (NOW DROP AND GIVE ME 20!)"

STRABERRY CAKE $16.99

[whispering] *"So be good . . ."*

". . . OR ELSE."

What, the angry Santas didn't scare your kids straight? Okay, new game plan: we'll show them how *disappointed* the big guy is when they shove crayons up little Austin's nose.

And you thought no one knew about the hamster incident. Tsk, tsk.

That's right, children:
kids who misbehave turn Santa's smile upside down.

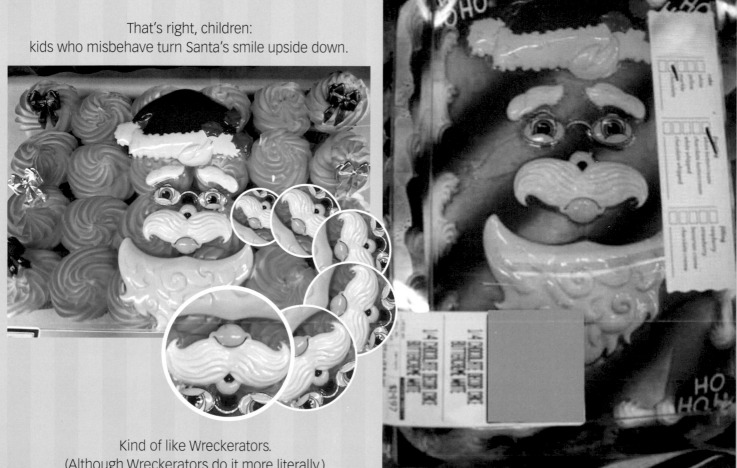

Kind of like Wreckerators.
(Although Wreckerators do it more literally.)

On the other hand, kids, if you're *good* then Santa might surprise you with one of his world-famous impressions!

Something like . . .

GEORGE CARLIN:

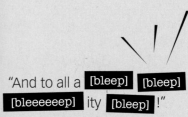

"And to all a [bleep] [bleep] [bleeeeeep] ity [bleep] !"

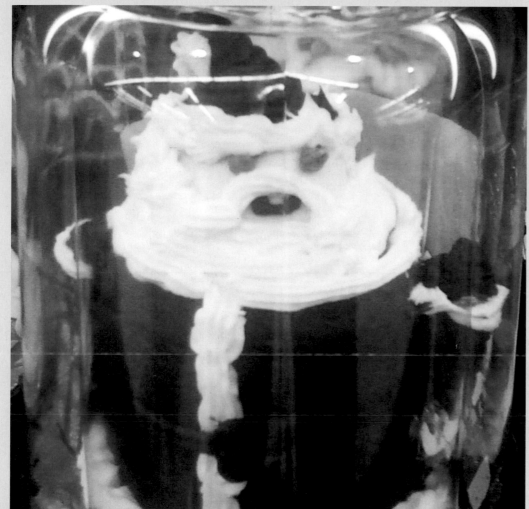

THE COWARDLY LION:

"Put 'em up, put 'em uuup!"

DAVY JONES:

(Er, that's the tentacle-face guy, not the Monkee.)

And Santa's pièce de résistance . . .

[drum roll, please!]

CONSTIPATED

Dude, Nick, maybe try some coffee
or something. You're about to put the
"pop" in "apoplexy."

That's right, kids, Santa can be *quite* entertaining—and sometimes in an adult, full-of-hot-air, dolled-up kind of way. (Putting the "b" in "subtle," that's me!)

Santa or Christmas Tree Party Cupcake $25.99

Yessir, you could say these Santas are crying out for commentary. Commentary that I, a wide-eyed innocent whose parents will be reading this book, cannot *possibly* provide.

Oh, don't look at me like that, Mrs. Claus. I didn't say *anything*.

Real Characters

Mini Tearaway Ca...
375g

While schools and religious and community organizations the world over strive to celebrate all the joy of the season, bakeries are fighting back the only way they know how: with an unfolding drama of tragedy, anger, and mutation—right there among the rye and pumpernickel.

First, let's set the scene with a nice crackling fire in the ol' fireplace:

See, I know this is a fireplace (and not Mount Vesuvius) because it says "fireplace" on the cake board. [tapping temple] *Nothing* gets past this steel trap here.

Next let's meet some of the characters in this month's pageant of poorly piped pastry.

Sure, she's a bit flaky,
but be careful;
GINGER SNAPS.

Then there's Earl, the patron saint of male pattern baldness:

That guy can really cut a rug.

Poopsie and *Flopsie* know how to bring the holiday cheer:

When they leave, everyone is MUCH more cheerful.

Humpty here likes to talk with his hands.

I would translate, but there are children present.

And let's not forget the Turdaphants!

These harbingers of Christmas "cheer" are perpetually puckered up, the better to suck your spirit dry with.

Of course, sometimes they *do* get a little carried away:

"Ah tink ah swa-woed mah own node. Hep."

[singing] But do you recaaall . . .

The most famous reindeer of all?

Poo-Dolph, the Bulldozed, Slain Deer!
Had some very wily foes,
And if you ever saw him,
You would pro'ly say, "How gross!"

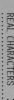

And because two heads are always better than one:

No, sorry, I take it back. They're not. They're really, really not. [shudder]

But, on the bright side, at least we know it can't get any creepier, right? Ha ha! Right?

What? Why are you all pointing behind me?

AAAAUUUUUGGGGHHHHH!!!

'Twas the Night Before Christmas

'Twas the night before Christmas,
when all through the house,
Not a creature was stirring,
not even a mouse.

So I guess those new
rat traps are working.

The stockings were hung by the chimney with care . . .

We'll, uh, just have to take your word for that.

"Rotten GPS. Oy, Blitzen! Where are we?"

The children were nestled all snug in their beds,

Ask for one more glass of water, kid, and those ropes get tighter.

While visions of sugar plums danced in their heads.

Uh . . .

Um . . .

Okay, *fine*. So I don't know what "sugarplums" are.

And Mama in her 'kerchief, and I in my cap,

Oh, like *you* don't wear a shearling cap and Elton John glasses to bed.

Had just settled our brains for a long winter's nap.

Braaaains.

When out on the lawn there arose such a clatter,
I sprang from the bed to see what was the matter!

Boops.

Away to the window I flew
   like a flash,
Tore open the shutters and threw up!

OH! Threw up the *sash*!

Sorry.

The moon on the breast of the new-fallen snow,

Remember those self-exams, ladies!

Gave the lustre of midday to objects below.

When, what to my wandering eyes should appear,

(Oh, was it 'wondering?' My bad.)

YULE LOG
$24.95

Plus a creepy Santa face, two snowmen heads, a white deer in a red cap, eight berries, four fake flowers, two tree sprigs, and fifteen plastic leaves. But hey, who's counting?

With a little old driver,
so lively and quick,

[crickets chirping]

I knew in a moment
it must be St. Nick!

He's *fine*, kids. Santa's just
taking a little nap. On the floor.
In the basement.

The smelly, smelly basement.

More rapid than eagles his coursers they came,

And he whistled, and shouted, and called them by name!

"Now, Dasher! Now, Dancer!
Now, Prancer and Vixen!

On, Comet! On, Cupid!
On, Donner and Blitzen!

"Okay, next time let's try to *avoid* dashing the snowmen."

As dry leaves that before the wild hurricane fly,

Oh yes, boys, *they're real.*

When they meet with an obstacle, mount to the sky.

It's ok; I'm pretty sure those are supposed to be peppermints.

With the sleigh full of toys,
and St. Nicholas, too.

Thank goodness for the North Pole label gun.

As I drew in my head, and was
turning around,
Down the chimney St. Nicholas
came with a bound.

"Uh, guys? A little help?"

He was dressed all in fur, from his head to his foot,
And his clothes were all tarnished with ashes and soot.

Actually, come to think of it, maybe that was Blitzen.

A bundle of toys he had
flung on his back,

Gee, Santa, you shouldn't have. Really.

And he looked like a peddler,
just opening his pack.

His eyes—how they twinkled!

His dimples how merry!

His cheeks were like roses,

Third degree roses.

his nose like a cherry!

A drunken, drunken cherry.

His droll little mouth was drawn up like a bow,

"That is the *last time* I pass out at the elves' office party."

And the beard of his chin
was as white as the snow.

"Do you hear me, elves? The *last time!*"

Uh, Santa has a prescription for that, kids.

And the smoke it encircled his head like a wreath.

Which is also how he landed those guest spots on *Lost*.

He had a broad face and
a little round belly,

Wait a minute. . . . Strike that.
Reverse it.

Thank you.

That shook when he laughed,
like a bowlful of jelly!

(Yeah. Ew.)

He spoke not a word, but went straight to his work,
And filled all the stockings, then turned with a jerk.

 Jerk.

And laying his finger aside of his nose,

Ah, so THAT's where it went.

"Diet . . . ooph! . . . starts . . . *tomorrow.*"

He sprang to his sleigh, to his team gave a whistle,
And away they all flew like the down of a thistle.

Or like a bunch of cupcakes connected by Twizzlers.
'Cuz it's hard to find a cake of a thistle.

But I heard him exclaim, 'ere he drove out of sight,

Eh, you get the idea.

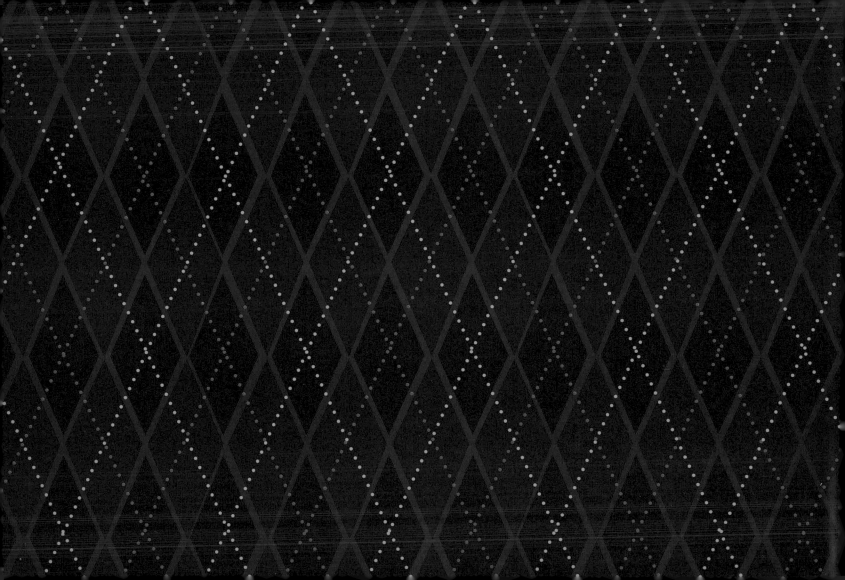

Now We're Eve'n'!

Well, my friends, another holiday season is drawing
to a close.

Soon we'll take time to reflect on the past twelve
months' memories and accomplishments, set new goals
for the future, and pick through our closets
in a vain attempt to find *something* that still fits.

But not yet.

No, before we can do any of that, we have to take out the
proverbial trash of the past year . . . and replace it with
the literal drunkenness of New Year's Eve. BOO-YA!

"You guys. Guys. Guys. GUYS. C'mere.
I just . . . I just wanna say. That. I. [sob]
LOVE. These nachos. [blowing nose on
sleeve] Anyway. To'lly drunk."

Of course, a successful New Year's Eve needs three things. Four things. No, five. Um . . .

Look, a successful New Year's Eve needs things. Things like:

1) Proper party attire.

Yeah. That's enough.

2) Booze.

Cleverly disguised as hot chocolate.

Or ham.

3) Pink elephants.

Don't ask.

Just blame Dumbo.

At least some of them bring their own tiny booze bottles.

Besides, there's nothing like a **pastel pink pile of pachyderm poo** to *really* get that party started.

And of course every good party should always *end* with:

4) A Big Bang

Bazinga.

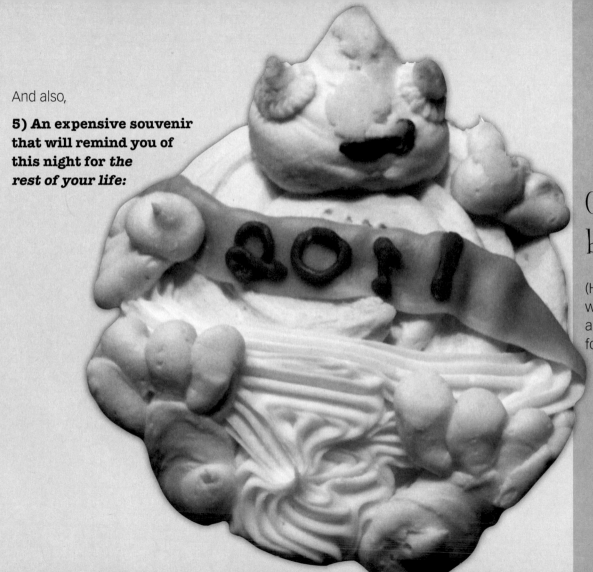

And also,

5) An expensive souvenir that will remind you of this night for _the rest of your life:_

2011

Or a freaky baby cake

(Hey, combine this sight with a bunch of tequila and see how soon _you_ forget it.)

Signs and Wonders

After finishing one of my books, people often ask me: "So Jen, do you *ever* leave the house?"

Ha ha! Such kidders, all of you.

Anyhoo, after that folks usually want to know how to avoid getting a wreck themselves. Where are the best places to shop? How can you tell? What's the best indicator?

Well, I know this sounds superstitious, but I like to look for a sign.

That'll do.

The first step is admitting you
need help.

Good job.

We would be happy to put a "Personal Greeting" on this cake!

"Personal Greetings" include:

"Thanks!"

I "love" you!

and

"Happy" "Birthday" "!"

ASK FOR ASSISTANTS

Merry Christmas

Specify blond or brunette at the register. (Sorry, redheads are on back order.)

Taste with our
Compliments

Please

Do not touch!

Sample

It wasn't easy breaking off that piece with my mouth, but I like to follow the rules.

So Long.
Goo Luck
and
THANKS FOR
ALL THE FISH!

And now, your moment of holiday Zen:

"Gingerbread is *people!*

GINGERBREAD IS PEOPLE!!!"